TWO GARDENS

Modern Hebrew Poems of the Bible

Translated by Jeff Friedman
and Nati Zohar

Foreword by Howard Schwartz

Acknowledgements

Our thanks to the publications in which these translations first appeared.

The Alembic: "Adam and Eve," "Eve Knew," "Leah," "Legacy," and "Rachel"

The Antioch Review: "The Binding," "Absalom," and "Autobiography"

Great River Review: "Jacob and the Angel," "A Man of Mystery," "Noah Afterwards," and "The Birth Chambers of the Ever Turning Sword"

Hayden's Ferry Review: "Isaac" and "Hagar"

Literary Imagination: "Two Gardens," "Potiphar's Wife"

Margie: "When God Said"

Pleiades: "Ararat"

Poetry International: "She Is Joseph" and "The Real Hero of the Story"

Perihelion: "Rachel" and "Eve"

"Ararat" was reprinted by *Poetry Daily*.

Cover Hamsa by Tsila Schwartz:

Published by Singing Bone Press
www.singingbonepress.com

Singing Bone Press

ISBN -10: 0933439113

Contents

Jacob and His Wives

Joseph

After Genesis

TWO GARDENS:
MODERN HEBREW POEMS OF THE BIBLE

FOREWORD

by Howard Schwartz

Where else but in Israel can so many bus riders be seen reading books of poetry? Nor are these readers limited to students—the love of poetry pervades Israeli culture. Poems are published in the weekend editions of the newspapers, and are widely read and discussed. The books of Yehuda Amichai, Israel's most popular poet, commonly sell ten thousand copies, and the first edition of his collected poems sold twice that number. Such sales figures are rare in this country, despite a reading public many times the size of Israel's.

What accounts for the widespread popularity of poetry in Israel? Surely it grows out of an almost universal knowledge of the Bible, which is a primary focus of Israeli education. After all, the language of Israel is the language of the Bible, and poetry has a central role in the Bible, not only in the Psalms and the Song of Songs, but scattered throughout the text, in key passages such as the Song at the Sea (Ex. 15:1-18). Hebrew poetry flourished in virtually every postbiblical period. So it is no exaggeration to say that poetry played a key role in keeping the Hebrew language alive over the long generations of exile, and that there is an unbroken tradition of Hebrew poetry from the time of the Bible to the present.

Perhaps no poems have had so great an impact on Jewish life as have the prayers. The prayers of the Siddur (prayerbook) and Machzor (holiday prayerbook) are drawn from the Bible, especially from the Psalms, from poems of medieval Hebrew poets such as Yehuda ha-Levi, Abraham ibn Ezra, and Shmuel ha-Nagid.

As this book demonstrates, there are an astonishing number of exceptional Hebrew poets. Of the older generation, there are Hayim Nachman Bialik, Nathan Alterman, and Uri Zvi Greenberg. Their work was largely formal, but in the next generation Yehuda Amichai used modern, colloquial Hebrew rather than biblical Hebrew as the language of his poems, and created a revolution in modern Hebrew poetry. Amichai towers above the all other contemporary Hebrew poets, but the tradition is greatly enhanced by poets such as Yona Wallach, Dan Pagis, Dalia Ravikovich, Haim Gouri, Natan Zach, Amir Gilboa, Natan Zach, Leah Goldberg, Rachel and Zelda. There are also some very impressive younger Israeli poets, such as Nurit Zarchi, who draw on the biblical wellspring. Her poem "She Is Joseph" is a daring commentary on the story of Joseph, proposing, convincingly, that Joseph was a woman disguised as a man.

The Hebrew poems that draw on the Bible continue an ancient, uniquely Jewish method of commentary known as the midrashic method. According to the ancient rabbis, God not only dictated the Torah (the first five books of the Bible) to Moses, he also explained it to him. Or as one 7th century midrashic text puts it, "God dictated the Torah to Moses during the day, and at night He explained it to him (*Pirqe de Rabbi* Eliezer). Exegesis comes from Sinai! In these midrashic texts the rabbis explained any problems or contradictions they encountered in the biblical text. And modern poets, writing in Hebrew, draw on this same method. So many of the poems collected in this book can be viewed not only as poems, but also as a kind of commentary. Take, for example, the poem "Isaac" by Amir Gilboa:

> Early in the morning,
> when the sun found us,
> my father gripped my hand.
>
> The knives glinted through the trees
> and the voices in the leaves
> called out for mercy.
>
> I was alone, waiting for you to find me.
> "Help me, father.
> Wherever I look, I see blood
> on the faces of the leaves, and everyone else
> has arrived at the noon meal."

Then they strangled his voice,
and breath left his lips, a star
opening in the blue waters of the sky.

And I cried out,
Tearing my eyes open, not wanting to believe,
but the forest had fallen away
and there was only smoke gathering
over the darkened tables
and a flower of ash on my window,
and my hand was empty.

On the literal level, this poem is a retelling of the biblical episode found in *Genesis* 22 of the binding of Isaac. But, unlike the biblical story, the victim here is not Isaac, but his father, Abraham. That is because the poem not only recalls the biblical episode, but also represents the generation of the fathers and mothers who died in the Holocaust, and Isaac represents their surviving sons and daughters. Thus the poem draws upon the biblical model and, at the same time, links it to a contemporary catastrophe, linking the past and present together.

In his poem "The Binding" Matti Megged also draws upon the story of Isaac to represent the fear and terror of Israeli soldiers fighting in one of their many wars. Here the biblical account provides no hope, but speaks bitterly of the meaningless of the endless wars:

When I was led again
to the sacrifice,
not on foot, not
on donkey—imprisoned
in an iron womb—
my father raised his arm,
but the angel didn't come down
to restrain him.

Alone,
father and son,
a wind sweeping through

drawing the curtain of dust,
my blood spilled
on the basalt, shining
darkly.

Above me, smoky skies
and the smell of my ashes
for centuries,
and from time to time
an old liar laughs
at my extinction.

In both cases, and in the other poems included that look back at the
biblical story, it serves as an archetype of the personal experience of
the poets. This demonstrates that the Bible is not a dead text, but a
living one, that can be called upon and reinterpreted in every
generation.

Sometimes a biblical episode can serve as the source for satire.
Consider Yehuda Amichai's poem "Jacob and the Angel:"

Before dawn she sighed
and seized him in that way and defeated him,
and he seized her in that way and defeated her,
and they could see a long wave coming to the shore.
In their holding they knew death,
but still she wouldn't say her name.

In the dawn light,
he saw her body—white
in the places that her swimsuit
had covered yesterday.

Later, they called down to her twice
as if calling a child
from her game in the sand
Then he knew her name
and let her go.

The biblical account (Gen. 32:22-31) tells how Jacob wrestled with a figure usually identified as an angel. Biblical commentaries offer a wide variety of reasons for this encounter, but when Jacob succeeds in wrestling the angel to a draw, the angel changes his name to *Yisrael*—one who wrestles with God. After that, Jacob leaves Jacob the Trickster behind, and becomes Jacob the Patriarch. Amichai's poem, set in the first person, describes the sexual wrestling of a man and a woman, a startling parallel to the profound biblical story that nevertheless sheds light and new meaning on the biblical account.

These poems all respond to the biblical source in their own ways. Like rabbinic Midrash, they not only draw upon the known—the biblical sources—but add personal interpretations that clearly demonstrate that the meanings of these biblical tales are endless and understood in many different ways. The portraits of God, of Adam and Eve, and the Garden of Eden are seen like the many facets of a jewel. In addition, the reader is treated to an exceptional collection of brilliant translations. Together Jeff Friedman and Nati Zohar translate these poems with exceptional clarity while retaining their poetic essence. The organization of the poems according to the biblical theme provides an opportunity to see how wide-ranging are the interpretations these Hebrew poets bring to the biblical text. Jeff Friedman is himself a major poet, the author of many of his own biblical poems. Nati Zohar demonstrates his remarkable ability to convey the poetic language in accurate and natural language. Jeff Friedman has recreated Nati Zohar's excellent literal translations into powerful lyrical poetry. Together they provide the reader with many profound surprises and delights.

The Garden of Eden

Two Gardens

Yona Wallach

If berries grew on you from head to foot,
I would pluck them with my teeth and eat them
one by one and then you would be naked,
your skin white and smooth. How hard
it is to feel naked and how beautiful, but there is
something ugly about naked flesh, so I say:
"The fruit here is not frightful
and misshapen. It is flowery and sweet—the fruit of Eden."
What are these tall winged creatures that scour the trails
and the trunks of trees? You tell me I'm afraid
the animals will find me. I suffer nausea before I give in
to curiosity, imagining something without limbs or blood.
Afterwards I run out, and the animals plunge
through the foliage, waving their bright tails.
Everything is soft and lovely. There are no seeds or thorns
in the garden, only lush vegetation and plump, luscious fruit.
But this garden will vanish and not one plant will blossom
as it did here. I'm afraid. My body is nothing
but air, and my soul hungers for the burning horizon.
Now we are surrounded by thorny plants, and our bodies
return to us as flesh and blood, sprouting nails and hair,
and odors rise from us as though we were damp earth.
The land confines us, but blood beats in the walls of our
          flesh,
though despair spreads its bright, bold colors. And
          afterwards,
we are again in the first garden, sweeter than any honey
you've ever tasted. I find you among the leaves
and call you my first love and now you see
I'm smooth as oil, lovely as a pearl.
But that garden is gone now, and here
a precise light dwells on our aging bodies.

When God Said for the First Time

Natan Zach

When the light fell, God wanted to open
his eyes, to see for the first time.
He didn't think, at that moment, about the blinding
sky or the trees that had already begun to
fill with water or the frightened birds
flying out of chaos. He didn't think about the words
he'd spoken in the dark, the animals stepping into
their wounded bodies. Then the first wind
touched God's eyes, who awoke in the cloud
of his dream and thought it was good.
He didn't think about Adam or Lilith or Eve
or Cain or Abel. He didn't think about the tribes
of men and women proliferating among the leaves,
who'd already begun to dream of themselves,
awake in the cities of the garden, their leaves
fallen, anguish stitched into their swollen hearts.
When God thought about night, he was dreaming.
"Like this, like this, I'll be blissful," he said.
"I am a good God." But fog thickened over the garden
and the fruit was weeping in the wet grass
and there were already too many to feed.

The Birth Chamber of the Ever-Turning Sword

Ronny Someck

God immerses the sunset in the clouds
and a fiery blue powder falls
over the earth.

Every creation story shatters
on the heavenly dance floor,
where a plane's shadow is pitched into the corners
like high heels tossed onto a cottony rug.

From the neck of the moon the keys dangle,
and no one can get into the rooms of thunder and lightning,
and no one can get in to the room where they paint
the decaying leaves on the tree of knowledge,
or to the birth chamber of the cherubim,
who turn their blades into flames.

Now the engines' rattle breaks
the quiet of the sky, drowning out
the baby born tonight and the moans that shake
loose the springs in the bedroom
where Adam and Eve lie.

Eve

Yaakov Fichman

I love Adam. Like God, he is wise
and generous, and his blood is precious,
but the serpent whispers his cruel thoughts in my ear
and his sweet breath passes over my body.

When Adam sleeps, rain douses the light
in the garden, and the birds grow silent and fearful.
He calls me from the bushes, he calls me from the leaves
and kindles a fire in my heart: "Taste it," he says, "taste it."

In the precise light of dawn, Adam's warm hand
caresses me, and he finds comfort on my breast
for he listens to the sound of my heart.

Yet every bush that reaches for the sun
leans to a different side at night, and the garden
is lush and lovely until night falls among the leaves.

The Serpent in Eve's Eyes

Shmuel Shatal

Brazen and slippery,
the serpent embraced her
with his long, sleek body,
and I didn't know
if the reflection in her eyes
was him or me.

I was there before anyone,
the first man, naming
each blossom, but she
was the shadow under the tree,
and I didn't know her
until now.

Eve Knew

T. Carmi

Eve knew what hid in the apple.
She wasn't born yesterday.
From the ribs of Adam
she oversaw the works of creation,
listening to the rustle of herbs and insects.

Eve knew what hid in the apple.
The waters raged, the moon blackened,
the letters raised their crowns,
the wild beasts preyed upon the names,
and the voice said: *It is good.*

Eve knew what hid in the apple:
a flowing stream of plants,
an exemplary garden, watered, saturated,
a righteous mother, happy
with every living thing.

Eve knew what hid in the apple.
To the light of day and with clear insight,
her naked body eclipsing the light of the sun,
she called out for freedom for the large worm
to chew at the roots of the trees.

In the end
Adam, his sweat flowing like a river,
confessed by the light of the sword
that he had run out of names, that his work
had sapped his strength

and that it was good.

Adam Explains His Silence

T. Carmi

I knew your body
even before I knew your name.
It was hard to speak.
The noise of creation was deafening,
stormy waters refused
to be torn apart, new wings struggled
in a nameless wind, moon facing
sun in great fury.
The depths cried; the barren trees
released zealous cries; a newborn thunder
burned after lightning; the sea was astounded
that a leviathan beats inside of it like a massive heart.

And when the wheel turned on us,
when the flaming sword spun,
there were no words left in my mouth.
I was so absorbed in the uproar
of the works of creation
that I knew your body
even before I knew your name,
still echoing somewhere in the garden.

Adam and Eve

Nurit Zarchi

We rose up from a single stem,
like an amaryllis that begins to die
if you cut its cup in two.
As with a blow
from the double axe of idol worshippers,
my love is severed.

Mixing thirst with poison,
I drink deeply
from the stream of memory,
letting it purify
my image of you.
You are without stain
as you wait for me in your pointed hat
and white coat—
my executioner.

I let you choke me until I can't cry out,
uncovering scars
red as roses,
blaming me again.
As a sign of victory,
you give me back the apple.
Our shadowy deal is cancelled.

I'm separating day
from night, my skin
from your skin, my lips
from the fruit
shiny
with our shame.

In a Beautiful Garden

Yehuda Amichai

A man sat in a beautiful garden,
half in light, half in memory.

His mother called him from a window of sleep,
but he wasn't sleeping and couldn't answer.

And he walked through the gate of the garden,
half himself, half someone else.

Now he remembers his first love,
but he's never returned to the garden,

and he lives with pleasure and pain,
and if he's not dead, he's still making love.

Cain and Abel

Autobiography

Dan Pagis

I died with the first strike and was buried
under the rocks, where no one would find me.
The raven taught my parents about death,
told them what to do with me.

My family still has a good name—and not a little
because of me. My brother invented murder.
My parents invented the black garment, grief.
I invented the other silence.

Everyone knows what happened.
Our inventions were perfected. One death led to another.
Decrees went out on blasts of air.
Those who murdered their own way
mourned their own way.

Out of respect for you,
I won't name all the names
for, at first, the details will horrify you,
but in the end, you'll grow tired and bored.

You can die once, twice, even seven times,
but you can't die a thousand times.
I can.
My underground cells reach everywhere.

As Cain multiplied on the face of the earth,
I multiplied in the belly of the earth,
my empire spreading like holes in the ground.
For a long time now my strength has exceeded his.
Everyday his armies desert and join me,
and this is only the beginning of my revenge.

Brothers

Dan Pagis

Supposedly, Abel was pure and modest
as a tender young kid,
wooly and full of curls
like the smoke of his offering
rising into the nostrils of God.
But Cain was straight
and sharp like a knife.

Cain was amazed. His large hand
felt inside the butchered throat—
Where does the silence begin?

Abel stayed in the field,
but it was decreed that Cain wander
and he wandered persistently
for years, moving from one
horizon to another
until one day he discovered
the earth had tricked him.
It moved under his feet,
but he went nowhere,
marching in place on a single
strip of dust,
no larger than his sandals.

On a beautiful evening
he found a bale of fine hay
and lay down in its cushion,
sinking into a blissful sleep.

God hushed all his creatures,
and while Cain slept, he dreamt
he was Abel, the chosen one,
"Don't be afraid," God said,
"for a sevenfold vengeance will fall on
the one who rises to kill you.
Don't be afraid—your brother Abel
protects you from evil."

Cain

Manfred Winkler

When he came to kill his brother
as though hunting a beast in the bright fields,
he had rehearsed this act so many times
he felt no anger or jealousy,
only the desire to accomplish the task
as precisely as possible.

Before he was born,
God whispered into the void
and created his future.
Then later He engraved the mark
on Cain's forehead to lead him
through the desert.

Cain obeyed too well, fulfilled
a slave's mission,
and God punished him
for not trying to rebel.
Therefore his deed contained
good and bad.

But he heard only the voice,
and not the silence,
aimed like an arrow at his heart.

The Flood

Ararat

Dan Pagis

After the ark plunges out of the water
and the survivors, in the chaos
of their happiness, burst
onto dry land, they dance
under the bluest sky they've ever seen,
shaking their hips and lifting their arms
and shouting for their prey.
And when the rainbow vaults across the sky
and the doves vanish into the light,
they know they've been saved.

But destruction comes to the impervious fish
who like sly speculators exploited the flood
for its great cargo of flesh.
Now on the hardened shore,
their exposed fins grow useless
and their open mouths gasp for air.

Noah Afterwards

Aryeh Sachs

Forty days cooped up
in a zoo is a long time,
but sometimes the waters
reflected sky
and the world seemed vast
and endless.
We couldn't eat meat,
because to kill only one
of the pairs of animals
would extinguish the flame
of a species. We ate
crabs, clams in season,
and a white fish
deep fried. And with each
meal we had the kind of wine
you could only get
back then—before the flood.
Ah, those were the days!
Why did He focus
on our sins when we had
so many admirable qualities?
We just wanted to enjoy
ourselves—why did
He get so angry?
We ate tomatoes from our garden,
ripe and red, the nectar
bursting from their silent skins.
We heard the cries
in the distance of the rain
like a ship without smoke,
sailing to nowhere.

It was just nice
reclining on the deck
with our bottle, watching
the sunset in the old world.
Now the fish wash up
on the slopes of Ararat,
suffocating in the sun
as the waters recede.
A shark is caught between
two boulders,
dying for his last meal.
But why does he smile?
Maybe, he's choking
in a rage of self pity.
Now there's nothing
but sun and more sun,
yet the perfume of herbs
doesn't mask the stink
of rotting flesh.
The end is so simple—
if you can forget.
Let him rot. Let him rot.
I won't grow tomatoes—I'll plant a vineyard.

A Cat in the Dovecot

Avner Treinin

He climbs up and seizes her.
There will be no olive branch delivered:
She won't fly back to the ark again.

Satisfied at last,
he glides on his velvet paws,
his knives cushioned
until he finds
a warm place to rest.

Outside a spatter of rain,
just a spatter.
There will not be another flood.

Abraham and His Wives

Abraham

Meir Wieseltier

Abraham loved only the one true God.
He despised the gods of other nations,
made of wood or clay, painted with lacquer.
He despised the idol maker who came home
every evening to his wife and devoured meat and wine,
who sold his wooden idols in the market like onions
and calculated his god and made himself the chosen one.

Of all the riches in the world, he loved only God.
He didn't bow to false gods. He said to the others
"Go about your business without me. I'll follow my own path,
and no one will ever say I exploited God."

He refused to take from anyone or give to anyone,
except God. He only had to ask
and he received anything he wanted, even a son, an heir.
But if there's a God, He wants what he wants,
and He also has an angel.

Abraham never sinned against God.
He couldn't. He was one with God,
not like Isaac, who loved his coarse-minded son,
not like Jacob, who worked for the sake of a woman,
who limped from the blows that God gave him at night,
who could only see the heavenly ladder in dreams.
With Abraham, God numbered the righteous in His cities
before they destroyed them.

Training on the Shore

Shlomo Vinner

They teach infants
to walk, soldiers
to crawl.
And between lessons
they show them the grains
of sand that God
showed Abraham
in the hour of the Covenant,
when he made him a nation
that would wander the desert.

They show them the sea
stricken by the moon,
the grass that sprouts
from the stones that were
once a wall of a temple.

And at midnight dew rises
from the beloved earth.
The stars bless the grass
sprouting from the stone,
and the grass blesses the stars
glittering over the sea.
They teach children
to walk, soldiers
to fall.

Hagar

Yokheved Bat-Miriam

She clasps her corals
around the neck of night and walks out
into the desert—small and silent.
The moon plunges through a wall of the water.

Like a tattoo twisting on her body,
she leaves her child and her lover.
A wind blows over the path,
white as divinity.

"I will never return to you, my country.
Like the Sphinx in the threshold of the sun,
I will remain here in the shimmering light,
in the glory of the desert, vast as fate.

In my mind I lie in the shade
of a cedar tree and the soft, moist
air soothes my eyes
and a song breathes over the bubbling well.

And with him who stayed on the other
side of this desert, who crossed
the boundaries of an unquenchable love,
starred with silence, parting and light,

who, in his heart, will never leave me,
I hide myself in delusion, in
drunken fantasy—childless
and alone.

Chased by his sleepless angels,

he will wander over the sands until he finds us
on his journey toward the sun and claims us as his,
for we are the kingdom of his dreams.

Stretch out your bow, my son.
The echo answers the arrow
to crown my pearly path,
to welcome me home.

Ishmael, Ishmael

Shin Shalom

Ishmael, Ishmael,
how long will this battle
rage between us?

My brother,
son of Hagar,
you are still wandering in the desert,
but you are not alone.

The same angel came to you
on your path through pain
as came to us on our road
through suffering.
If only we could hear each other,
as we heard the voice of the angel.

The caravan never stops,
marching reluctantly
from life to death,
and we've both seen God
hovering in the heat.

The grass is dry as straw.
The mushrooms are bursting
everywhere.
Put down your stone, Ishmael,
and I'll put down mine,
and then we'll find
the well where our children
can drink deeply.

Sarah

Manfred Winkler

At the entrance to the tent
she heard the messenger's
wild decree and laughed,
for she couldn't believe,
even with the miracles she had witnessed.

But she was startled:
The voice descended, filling her house,
and his powerful wings spread above.
She lied, because the truth
was a denial of his strength,

She knew the reason for her weakness,
the secrets of her aging body.

"No!" he raised his voice,
"You laughed" and then
he pronounced a law against
every lie.

She bowed her head
and couldn't see his knowing smile,
forgiving her and himself—
and she left the tent—
a grain in his hand.

The Binding of Isaac

Isaac

Amir Gilboa

Early in the morning,
when the sun found us,
my father gripped my hand.

The knives glinted through the trees
and the voices in the leaves
called out for mercy.

I was alone, waiting for you to find me.
"Help me, father.
Wherever I look, I see blood
on the faces of the leaves, and everyone else
has arrived at the noon meal."

"It's my blood, my son."

Then they strangled his voice,
and breath left his lips, a star
opening in the blue waters of the sky.

And I cried out,
tearing my eyes open, not wanting to believe,
but the forest had fallen away
and there was only smoke gathering
over the darkened tables
and a flower of ash on my window,
and my hand was empty.

In the Beginnings

Yehudit Kafri

In our dim beginnings
one story blazes out:
a father, his son
and the knife.
Where was Sarah?
How could she
have let it happen?
How could she have depended
on a God so ruthless
to save Isaac
at the last moment?
Why didn't she stop her husband
when he bound the donkey
and loaded the wood,
when she saw
there was no other
animal to sacrifice?
Why didn't she block his path,
her teary eyes glistening,
and whisper through loving lips,
"You will have to murder me first
before I let you take this child we waited for
a hundred years—this child
who is our life."

Legacy

Haim Gouri

The ram was caught in the thicket,
but Abraham didn't know that it had come
as an answer to the boy's question,
giving him strength in his darkest moment.

The old man raised his head,
and when he saw the angel standing there
and knew he wasn't dreaming,
the knife fell from his hand.

Free of his bonds,
Isaac watched his father turn away,
humbled,
his shoulders trembling.

The way it is told, Isaac lived
many years, took what pleasures
life had to give,
until the light was extinguished from his eyes.

But at that hour he bequeathed to his sons
a knife in the heart.

The Sacrifice

Matti Megged

When I was led again
to the sacrifice,
not on foot, not
on donkey—imprisoned
in an iron womb—
my father raised his arm,
but the angel didn't come down
to restrain him.

Alone,
father and son,
a wind sweeping through
drawing the curtain of dust,
my blood spilled
on the basalt, shining
darkly.

Above me, smoky skies
and the smell of my ashes
for centuries,
and from time to time
an old liar laughs
at my extinction.

Binding

Yehuda Amichai

To bind is to tie
and one can also tie
with ropes of love
on an altar sweeter
than any bed.

And that is my good angel
with her silky ropes, tearing
off her dress, my good angel
ready on the carpet—
only sixteen.

And as I rise
the light bathes her cheeks,
and a voice comes
down from the ceiling,
"Don't lay your hand."

"You ruin everything," the girl says
and unties her knot.

The Real Hero of the Binding

Yehuda Amichai

The real hero of the binding was the ram,
who stumbled innocently into the thicket
and didn't know about the plot
to sacrifice him in place of Isaac.
I want to praise his curly wool
and the depths of his human eyes
and the horns that were quiet while he lived.

And after he was slaughtered,
they turned them into shofars
and sounded their call to battle,
and their obscene cries of pleasure.

I want to remember the last moment
like a beautiful photo in an elegant fashion magazine,
the boy tanned and delicate in his velvet robe
and next to him the angel dressed in shimmery silk,
the boy and the angel waiting
with empty eyes—across from them
two empty spaces.

And behind them, in the colorful background,
a moment before his slaughter,
the ram caught the thicket, his last hope,
with his horns.

After, the angel flew back to heaven,
and Isaac set out looking for home,
trailing Abraham and God
who had left long
before, but the ram—

the real hero of the story—
stayed behind.

At the Tomb of the Patriarchs

Bracha Serri

Aliza says
that everyone who went to pray
at the Tomb of the Patriarchs
is crying for Sarah,
who has lost so many children.
"We are all," she says
"older than our years, alive
in the great double womb
of the feud between the brothers,
battling for the birthright,
for the land.
"No, " I say, "I have
remained a girl with Isaac
and for me, he never rose
from the altar of the sacrifice.
And I have remained in the desert
with Hagar and her child Ishmael,
thirsty and parched,
searching for a well
that is not dry
to give water to the boy.
And I have remained a slave, a refugee,
fleeing my love, my land,
a mistress of frozen feeling,
persecuted and tortured
but without hatred,
and I have remained a Jewess
without identity, without a voice,
barren in the blazing sun."

The Sacrifice

Aliza Shenhar

Amidst the fires
the loudspeaker shrieks,
"Give us your only son,
the one you love."
The altar is ruined. The wood
from the sacrifice is scattered.
The young men kick the ball
downfield for their loves,
their tongues hot. But now
the knife glints
in the valley, and the moon
flares over the paths to the border.
The white angel, the one
who cries out to each father,
"Don't raise your hand,"
is on vacation.

Sacrifice

Eliezer Cagen

I took my son, my only son,
to Moriah,
as I was commanded,
and plunged a knife into his neck
and offered him as a sacrifice
to a jealous, vengeful god.

And no heavenly voice descended.
And no hand grasped mine
to stop the knife
from killing my son.
And no ram appeared
to appease God.

Angels and princes, presidents and their staffs,
came to honor him.
I tore my clothing, tied
rags to my body with a belt.
First among the mourners,
I marched through the field,
leading my son
to his burial.

And the whole nation, from elders
to young boys and girls,
cried for him, for us.
And though his death didn't
purify our hearts nor cleanse
us of our sins, I sacrificed him—
seized by a great madness.

Jacob and His Wives

Jacob and the Angel

Yehuda Amichai

Before dawn she sighed
and seized him in that way and defeated him,
and he seized her in that way and defeated her,
and they could see a long wave coming to the shore.
In their holding they knew death,
but still she wouldn't say her name.

In the dawn light,
he saw her body—white
in the places that her swimsuit
had covered yesterday.

Later, they called down to her twice
as if calling a child
from her game in the sand.
Then he knew her name
and let her go.

The Smell of the Fields

Haim Gouri

Esau, the heat is relentless,
and there is no shade
anywhere
as you descend the basalt path
to the sweltering fields.
Today you are not too wise
and not too holy,
and the smell of sweat, smoke, and goats
wraps you in a cloud.

There is sadness in you,
but also the strength
that comes from the dust,
the stones, the metals of the earth.
When you are needed, when you are called,
you come.

The heat is relentless,
but you've been chosen
to do the black work. Someone
has to do it. Someone
has to run and return
the stolen goods, and that someone
is you.

You'll never rest—we won't let you,
because you're so strong, so misguided.
Esau, someone is always less loved,
unworthy of our mercy.

Rachel

Rachel Blusten

She is the blood that flows in my blood.
She is the voice that sings in my voice—
Rachel, shepherdess of Laban's flock,
Rachel, mother of mothers.

Therefore the walls of this house are narrow
and the city is strange,
for her scarf once fluttered
in the desert wind.

Therefore I will take up my path
with the confidence of Rachel, for the distances
she traveled, for the memories of the wide, warm sands,
are written on the soles of my feet.

Rachel

Haim Gouri

She comes to me in darkness for love
and I don't know who she is
or how she came to be called Rachel.
She's beautiful, but her face
is not like the face in one of those exquisite portraits,
not like the face of the woman touching
the strings of the harp in the pale gold light.

And my Rachel lies with me and wanders in me until dawn,
but when the morning rises, she is Leah.

And for me she is my darling Leah, whose eyes
fill with tenderness when she looks at me
and for me she is Rachel, for whom I struggled so many
years.

And now she has departed from my arms, my touch,
and my death rises over the horizon.

And I shall never find another like Rachel,
who has witnessed my weakness and my worst crimes.
She is the wind hovering over the water
and the letters carved in the sacred stone.

I cover my face and remain in silence
but I am naked and unmasked.

And all that remains is a small thin voice
and the raven that sits on the stone
and the hand that remembers her body
and her name.

Like Rachel

Moshe Dor

To die like Rachel
while your soul trembles,
longing for escape,
while your life turns over
inside you like a baby
waiting to be born—

and outside the tent
Jacob and Joseph cry for you,
their bodies trembling.

How painful—
to feel Jacob's love
eating you from within.
Now as your soul rises,
the baby gurgles and cries

and Jacob enters the tent,
but you can't see him,
nor can you feel his breath on your lips.
The midwife whispers a blessing
bathing your face and body.

The calm air rests on your cheek.
Your breath won't stir a feather.
They bury you among
the stones of the mountain,
but no words can comfort them.
O God, let me die like Rachel.

Hard Water

Moshe Dor

We have hard water,
hard soil, hard
stars, hard people.
You entice us with soft
water, soft soil,
soft stars, you seduce us
with soft women.

When Jacob struggled
with the angel, his feet trampled
hard soil. Hard water
shined in the ditches.
Hard stars fell,
caught in his stiff
tangled beard.

He was down, in the grip
of defeat, until the angel,
in a voice torn by
weariness, told him
of Rachel's soft breasts,
her slopes of honey.

Then all at once, twelve stones
fused into the pillow he
laid under his head, twelve tribes,
and he saw the hard white path
through the desert that would
lead him to Canaan. Not
even his thigh, wounded
by the angel, would stop him

from reaching the promised land—
the hard land.

Leah

Aryeh Sivan

Leah was tired.
In the evening she sat and stared
at a burning candle and counted
the drops of nectar streaming down.
Around her the tribe of children played
and there were too many for her to recall their names.
Surely everything that came
had to come
and everything that had to be,
came.

They never believed she hadn't
used the darkness to deceive,
hadn't tried to conceal her
flawed, naked body, nor would they believe
her eyes were tender from crying.

The spirit had gone from her.
She was too tired to retell the story again
and why would she retell it now?
Instead she told herself that she loved
her husband, and that the touch of his flesh
kindled a flame inside her
and redeemed her.

There was, of course, some truth in this.
In every lie there is some truth
and besides her story was so tangled
over the years that it was woven
into a dense cloth—
a knot in the throat.

Joseph

She Is Joseph

Nurit Zarchi

Rachel knots her daughter's hair
and presses it down under a silk cap
and chalks her face to roughen the skin
and calls her Joseph.

For she has no son
and her prayers are numbered
and she must lie to her husband, to her husband's sons.
She must lie even to God.

The little girl sits in the tent
in an opulent blue gown
and in public, she is Joseph,
but in private her mother brushes her abundant hair.

Now Rachel has given Israel
an heir, Joseph, the beautiful one,
and has washed away her disgrace
as though bathing her daughter's innocent thighs.

She lifts off the silk cap
and unknots the abundant hair
and lets it fall
over her daughter's delicate shoulders

and reads the future in its darkness.
"My daughter, your brothers will cast you
into a pit and then sell you into slavery."
The young girl sits in the tent

drinking the shadows with her eyes,
caught in the spell of her mother's hands,
in the spell of her words, in the story she is weaving
out of the sheen of her hair.

Shaken, Rachel says, "But that is not all.
You will be locked in a prison
because of your dreams,
yet only your dreams can save you.

My prayers are numbered, and I can't
decipher the words in the water, and a prophecy hovers
in the wind that passes over the fallen sheaves
and the dying kine."

The little girl sits in the tent,
afraid to breathe,
and her mother holds her hair
and calls her Joseph.

The Stripes in Joseph's Coat

Rivkah Miriam

The stripes in Joseph's coat
were like the rungs in the ladder in Jacob's dream.
When he walked in the fields,
the coat was warmed
by the sun, the moon and the stars.
The sheaves fell at his feet.

In the pit he curled up
in the arms of his mother, Rachel of the well.
Above, the Ishmaelites roamed through the desert,
the bells around the necks of their animals ringing.
And Joseph was carried on the hump of a camel
as though in the heart of the sea.

The camel rolled back its long, sleek neck.
The arms of the woman beckoned,
and the bracelets glinted in his eyes.

Rachel sat on the camel, concealing the idols,
pressing them to her like large dolls.

But Joseph touched them
and they pierced him with their fingers,
ordering him to Egypt.
His God slept under him
like a pillow formed from tribes of stones.

Potiphar's Wife

Yehudit Kafri

What really happened
between Joseph and Potiphar's wife?
What canal did he dig for her
in the desert?
What secret blue water flowed between them?
Maybe he blew his words gently into her ear
or maybe his eyes told her.
A woman doesn't simply ask a man
to sleep with her. Something
happened between them,
but the Bible doesn't tell.
Sure, Joseph was thrown into a pit.
Sure, he suffered, but he always
climbed to the top.
This dreamer of dreams,
who reached the highest position in Egypt,
was so practical he sold
his people as slaves to Pharaoh,
sold even the fields and cattle.
He gained wealth and power
and married Asenath,
daughter of the high Priest of On.
He was a respected man, apparently,
but what happened to Potiphar's wife
when she was found in bed
with his robe in her hands?
What happened when she was left
with Potiphar?
I can't even begin to tell,
though I know.

After Genesis

Moses

Amir Gilboa

I came up to Moses and said,
"Deploy the troops like this."
He praised me
and did what I told him.

And who didn't see my glory then?
Beautiful Sarah from my childhood was there—
I wanted to build a city in her name.
And there was the girl with long legs from the workers' farm
and Dina from the Italian-Yugoslavian border
and Riyah from the lowlands in the North.

Proudly I showed Moses
the right path, and then I realized that she,
whose name is engraved
precisely in the seal of my own name,
wasn't there.

Moses, Moses, lead our people
through this wilderness,
for I'm still a boy
and must sleep now.

And the Whole Nation Saw

Miriam Rivka

They saw the voices coming toward them,
sparks of fire, smoke,
but they hoped the voices couldn't see them.
"Moses," they said, "tell us what God says
for if God speaks to us,
we will be consumed by His words."

With his veined hands
Moses reached out to them,
and like a fiery canopy, the voices rested on his hands,
and his hands grew heavy.
Then Israel saw the voices
in his tangled beard, in his hungry mouth
in the bright words burning on his lips.

A Man of Mystery

Dahlia Rabikovich

Aaron is dark and mysterious,
a deep stream.
He's not like other men.
Sometimes he thinks he's God
since his Grandfather was a man of God.
He has a lovely voice
and sings in the morning.
He has so many thoughts
that in the sun patio he gets lost
among all the plants.
The sun brightens the leaves,
and the sugary leaves shine like phosphorus.
He says it's warm even at night,
but he doesn't always speak the truth.
More than anyone he gets lost in the desert,
wandering over the sand.
Sometimes others think he is dead.
He has just gone far away.
Distance doesn't scare him.
Nothing scares him,
except the needle in the vein.
I know him better than anyone.
I was with him when he died.

Miriam

Yoheved Bat-Miriam

She stood among the reeds and papyrus
and breathed in the desert.
A brilliant blue flooded
the sleeping eyes of stars
and streamed over the desert's murmuring,
over the dialogue of hieroglyphs,
over the song marching from
the glittering doors of the palace.

At a distance in the fertile ground of memory,
like a horned snake in eternal lust,
trampled Goshen emerged
from the skin of its cocoon, coaxing
her back into the dim tribal imagination.

ɪ am with you in the storm,
your body curving like a drum,
with you as you whirl into fervor,
into the smell of sand and eternity.

"I speak out of jealousy,
out of disfiguring disease, out of self-hatred,
but still I adjure you in your relentless asceticism
to remain on your lonely peak,
dazzling as a desert."

As the white foam of the waves whispered,
she rocked back and forth
looking down on the baby
in her arms like a vow,
like a decree, like redemption,
like fate.

Joshua's Face

Amir Gilboa

Joshua looks down at me,
and his face is beaten gold
as in a dream where he is embalmed.
When I walk out,
the ocean strikes the shore eternally,
and I'm so grief-stricken by its lament,
I might die tonight.
But I'm forced to wait here, forced
to remain alive.
My brother's face rises in the dark
to foretell my footsteps in the cold sand.

The ocean strikes and withdraws,
strikes and withdraws—
the wars of nature dictated by law.
But me, I'm different, running
away in the wind, far away…
 My Joshua also rests now from war.
He left the land to his people,
but he didn't carve a tomb for himself
in the mountains of Ephraim.
Night after night
he still wanders the sky alone, looking for his home,
and I'm so grief-stricken
I might die tonight, walking barefoot
in the cold sand on the edge of the ocean,
where my fate roars—wave after wave
striking my feet.

Joshua, high above us,
may you be praised and loved.

Saul

Amir Gilboa

I don't know if it was shame, Saul,
or fear of the spirit you summoned,
but on the walls of the Bet-Shean
I turned away.

Then after refusing to carry your sword,
I stood mute,
and blood trickled from my heart.
I don't really know if I'm your child,
but I'm here, waiting with the others.

And you are our king,
our honored king, calling us to war.

And I really don't know
how to tell you who I am
or why I'm in this place.

Saul, come back!
In Bet-Shean, your children
are waiting.

Absalom

Yona Wallach

I must again remember
my son Absalom,
whose hair caught in my uterus,
and I couldn't give him enough
to make him whole.
I am building a shore for my emotions,
where pity washes over me
and the possibilities of hunger.
I must remember my poor Absalom,
alone on the shore,
who never had a chance
to fulfill his legacy.
In another life
I pray Absalom will be my lover,
and I will only sense the memory
of my empty womb—
my son like a constellation
of stars, falling.
But even in another life, I will remember
how the sword hit
the magnet of my heart.
Pain is always precise:
What will you fight for,
and on what will you rest,
and where will the wind
send you, my son.

Samson

Amir Gilboa

Samson grows old,
and his dreams wander the night.

As a child he lifted the world on its axis
with one hand. As a young man
he asked to die on the night
of his seventeenth birthday.

He didn't want to die
old. He caught 300 foxes,
and fastened torches to their tails
and watched the fires in their wake
burning up the grain and the olive trees.
In his twenties, he wanted to perform heroic deeds
until the day of his death, at thirty-three.

When they gouged out his eyes,
he prayed to see his daughters' weddings.
Now, in the oblivion of his hours,
it's as though he's eighty and unformed
and still he dreams like a baby.

And still the gates of his hell slumber in their power.
And Delilah. . . .

Biographical Notes for the Poets

Yehuda Amichai was born in 1924 in Germany and emigrated to Palestine in 1936. His work has been translated into thirty-seven languages, including Chinese, Estonian, and Albanian. Considered one of the most important Hebrew poets of the twentieth century, he is the recipient of numerous awards, including the Israel Prize, his country's highest honor. He died in 2000.

Yoheved Bat-Miriam (1901 - 1980) was born in Belorussia and settled in Eretz Israel in 1928. Her first volume of poetry, published in 1932, was followed by six other collections. She was awarded the 1964 Bialik Prze and the 1972 Israel Prize.

Rachel Blusten (1890-1931) was born in Vyatka in Russia and arrived in Eretz-Israel at the age of 19. She first worked as a laborer in Rehovot and later joined a training farm near the Kinneret. Eventually she settled in Tel-Aviv, where most of her poems were written during the last six years of her life. She published two books of her poems during her lifetime, *Safiah* and *Mineged*. Her collected poems was published posthumously in 1935 and has since appeared in many editions.

Eliezer Cagen (1914-2000) was born in Russia, and moved to Israel in 1935. He was an Israeli poet, translator, educator, and researcher of literature. He published ten books of poetry. He was awarded the Shin Shalom Prize in Literature for his life work in Hebrew poetry.

T. Carmi (1925-1994) grew up in New York and studied at Yeshiva University and Columbia University. He published his first poems in Hebrew while still living in the U.S. He immigrated to Eretz Israel in 1947. In addition to publishing numerous volumes of his own poems, he translated and edited two volumes of Hebrew poetry, including *The Penguin Book of Hebrew Poetry*.

Moshe Dor Born in Tel Aviv in 1932, he has published forty works of poetry in Hebrew, and his poems have been translated into some thirty languages.

Yaakov Fichman (1881-1958) was an acclaimed Hebrew poet, essayist, and literary critic. He emigrated to Palestine in 1919, where he lived until his death. His poetry followed a traditional lyric Romantic style. He was awarded the Israel Prize for Literature in 1957.

Amir Gilboa (1917-1984) was considered one of the major poets in Israel. He published numerous volumes of poetry and won many of Israel's most prestigious literary prizes.

Haim Gouri worked in DP camps with Jewish survivors following WWII and fought in the 1948 War of Independence. Gouri, a journalist and novelist, is best known as a poet. He has received many literary awards, including the Bialik Prize and the Israel Prize.

Israeli poet **Yehudit Kafri** has published eight volumes of poetry, a memoir and several children's books. She was the recipient of the Rachel Prize in 1993.

Matti Megged (1923-2003) was born in Poland, and emigrated with his family to Israel at the age of 3. He is the author of *The Animal that Never Was* and *Dialogue in the Void*.

Rivka Miriam is an Israeli poet, writer, and painter. She was born in Jerusalem in 1952. She has published twenty three books of poetry, as well as several children's books. Many of her poems are part of the required high school curriculum of the Israeli Department of Education.

Dan Pagis (1930-1983): During his lifetime, Dan Pagis published many volumes of poetry and is considered, along with Yehuda Amichai, one of the most important Hebrew poets of the twentieth century. Pagis was also a scholar of medieval Hebrew literature at Hebrew University.

Dahlia Ravikovitch (1936-2005) Awarded the Israel Prize and the Bialik Prize for her poetry, Dahlia Ravikovitch was considered to be one of the leading poets of the generation that came of age with the creation of the state of Israel, a generation that included Yehuda Amichai, Dan Pagis, and Natan Zach.

Aryeh Sachs (1932-1992), born in Tel Aviv, was an Israeli poet, translator, editor, and screenwriter. He also served as a professor at the Hebrew University of Jerusalem.

Born in Yemen, **Bracha Serri** writes political and feminist poetry that also draws heavily on the linguistic and metaphoric tradition of the great Yemenite religious poets such as Shalom Shabazi. Her books include *The Sacred Cow* (1991), *Red Heifer* (1990), and *Seventy Wandering Poems* (1983).

Shin Shalom (1904-1990) was an Israeli poet, writer, and translator. He was born in Poland and emigrated with his Hasidic family to Israel in 1922. He published many works of autobiographical prose and poetry, and his poems have been translated in multiple languages. He was awarded the Israel Prize for Poetry in 1973.

Shmuel Shatal was born in Russia in 1913. He emigrated to Israel in 1929, where he studied engineering at the Technion. He has written poetry, prose, literary criticism, as well as translations.

Aliza Shenhar was born in 1943 in Tiberias, Israel. She formerly served as the Rector of the University of Haifa. Her main field of research is the uses of folklore and folktales in literature and drama. She has taken over the Israel Folktale Archives from its founder, her teacher, Professor Dov Noy.

Aryeh Sivan fought in Israel's War of Independence as a member of the elite Palmach unit. He has published 8 collections of poetry and a novel. His poetry has been widely translated.

A leading Israeli poet, **Ronny Someck** has published eight books of poetry, two books of translations and a book for children which he co-authored with his daughter, Shirly. He has received the ACUM Special Jubilee Prize, the Prime Minister`s Prize and the Amichai Prize. His poetry has been translated into 22 languages.

Avner Treinen (1928-2011), born in Tel Aviv, was an Israeli poet and a Professor of Chemistry at the Hebrew University of Jerusalem. He published several books of poetry and chemistry textbooks. He was a member of the Academy of the Hebrew Language.

Shlomo Vinner was born in Jerusalem in 1937. He has published several books of poetry and translation, and his poems have been published in important anthologies in Hebrew and English. He also serves as a Professor of Mathematics at the Hebrew University of Jerusalem.

Yona Wallach (1944-1985) was one of the leading avant-garde poets in Israel. During her lifetime she published three volumes of poetry, and collections of her poetry continue to be published posthumously. In 1978, she won the Israeli Prime Minister's Literary Prize for her poetry. Wallach also wrote lyrics for rock bands who appeared with her at poetry readings/musical performances.

Meir Wieseltier is a prize-winning Israeli poet. He has published thirteen volumes of poetry, and was awarded the Israel Prize for Literature and Poetry in 2000.

Manfred Winkler (1922-2014) was born in the Ukraine, and emigrated to Israel in 1959. He published works of poetry and prose in German and Hebrew, and also was a translator and sculptor. He was awarded the Israel Prize for Literature in 1999.

Natan Zach was born in Berlin in 1930 and moved to Israel with his family when he was six. He has published some eight collections of verse, several volumes of prose, and children's literature.

Nurit Zarchi was raised on a kibbutz in Israel. A pronounced feminist, Zarchi is a poet, essayist, novelist and author of books for young readers, She is considered one of the leading voices in contemporary postmodern Israel fiction and children's literature.

The Translators

Jeff Friedman has published six poetry collections, five with Carnegie Mellon University Press, including *Pretenders*, *Working in Flour*, and *Black Threads*. He has co-translated with Dzvinia Orlowsky *Memorials: A Selection* by Polish Poet Mieczyslaw Jastrun. For their translations, Friedman and Orlowsky were awarded a National Endowment Literature in Translation Fellowship for 2016.

Nati Zohar lives in San Rafael, California, where he is an entrepreneur. He served as a combat soldier in the Israel Defense Forces and lived in Israel for eleven years, before making California his home. This is his first published work of translation.